What

Nintendo?

by Gina Shaw

illustrated by Andrew Thomson

Penguin Workshop

To Micah, Louisa, and Samantha, may your creativity bring joy to others!—GS

For Rhia,
and for Cerys—welcome to the world—AT

PENGUIN WORKSHOP
An Imprint of Penguin Random House LLC, New York

Published by Penguin Workshop, an imprint of Penguin Random House LLC, New York.
PENGUIN and PENGUIN WORKSHOP are trademarks of Penguin Books Ltd.
WHO HQ & Design is a registered trademark of Penguin Random House LLC.
Printed in the USA.

Visit us online at www.penguinrandomhouse.com.

Library of Congress Cataloging-in-Publication Data is available upon request.

ISBN 9780593093795 (paperback) 10 9 8 7 6 5 4 3 2 1
ISBN 9780593093801 (library binding) 10 9 8 7 6 5 4 3 2 1

Contents

What Is Nintendo?

In 1979, an engineer who worked at Nintendo was taking a long train ride. His name was Gunpei Yokoi (say: GUN-pay YO-koh-ee). On the trip, he noticed a passenger playing with a calculator, pressing all the buttons on it. Gunpei was fascinated. At that time, Nintendo made large-size arcade games with big joysticks. But it suddenly struck him that a handheld gaming device might also be fun. So, he brought his idea to the president of Nintendo.

Did he like the idea?

Yes, a lot!

Right away, Gunpei and his team started to develop the Game & Watch. It was the perfect time for this—liquid crystal display (LCD) technology had become inexpensive, and video games were now big business.

The finished product could fit in a child's hand. It had only one game that was played on a screen. The Game & Watch was cheap, and had a long battery life. Most important of all, the game was fun to play.

The first Game & Watch game was *Ball*, and it was sold around the world. Gunpei had done it! The Game & Watch was a major success.

Game & Watch game called *Ball*

Between 1980 and 1991, Gunpei's team created sixty different Game & Watch devices.

Gunpei Yokoi worked from a single, simple idea. Because of his creative ability, he helped Nintendo make history in the video game industry.

What's in a Name?

The name *Nintendo* comes from three Japanese kanji characters: 任 天 堂. They are *nin*, *ten*, and *do*. Kanji is a Japanese system of writing that adapted characters from Chinese writing. These three kanji characters are part of Nintendo's original corporate logo. A logo is a symbol that is created to identify a company and that appears on its products. Nintendo's name means loosely "leave luck to heaven."

CHAPTER 1
All in the Family

Fusajiro Yamauchi

Nintendo was founded in Kyoto, Japan, all the way back in 1889 by Fusajiro Yamauchi (say: foo-SAH-ji-ro YAH-ma-oo-chi). Fusajiro was a wood-block printer and artist. His new company made beautiful playing cards called *hanafuda*.

(The name comes from a combination of the Japanese words for *flower* and *card*.) The cards were made from tree bark. The ink for the designs was made from flower petals and berries.

At this time in Japan, the government banned all playing cards because gambling was against the law. And many card games involved gambling. After a while, though, the government let Nintendo sell its cards because they didn't have numerals and were so beautiful.

In each deck of hanafuda cards, there are twelve suits—each named for a month of the year and a flower. Each suit contains four cards, making a total of forty-eight cards. Many different card games can be played with hanafuda cards.

The cards sold well in Japan but nowhere else.

So, Nintendo remained a medium-size playing card company. To become bigger, it would need to head in new directions.

Sekiryo Kaneda Yamauchi

In 1929, after forty years as president of Nintendo, Fusajiro Yamauchi retired. His daughter had married a man who had been adopted by Fusajiro. His name was Sekiryo Kaneda Yamauchi (say: SE-ki-ryo KA-ne-da YAH-ma-oo-chi), and he was the next president of Nintendo.

When Sekiryo took over Nintendo, it was the largest playing card company in Japan. In his twenty years as president, he made Nintendo much more efficient by introducing an assembly line of workers and building a large sales force and factory. He retired in 1949 and chose his twenty-two-year-old grandson to run the company.

Hiroshi Yamauchi (say: HEE-row-shi YAH-ma-oo-chi) had been raised by his grandparents from the time he was five. He had a difficult childhood. His grandparents were very strict. To prepare him to become the next president of Nintendo, they sent him to a school where he would study either law or engineering. But World War II interrupted his grandparents' plans.

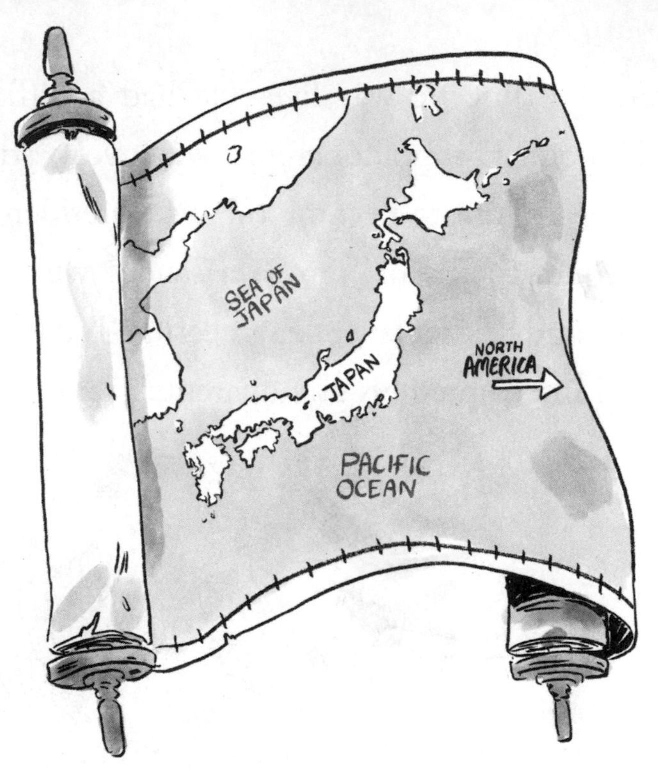

In 1939, when Hiroshi was twelve years old, the Japanese government forced him to quit school. World War II was raging. Hiroshi was too young to fight. Instead, he had to work in a military factory for several years. After the war ended in 1945, he studied to become a lawyer. But he left law school when his grandfather chose him to take over Nintendo.

From the start, Hiroshi was a strong and bold leader. He took the job only after being told that he could fire his relatives at Nintendo. Why was that important to him? He wanted to make sure that no one in the company thought he was favoring his family. And he also didn't want any relatives challenging his authority. His grandfather did not like this idea, but he agreed to it.

Many workers didn't think Hiroshi had enough experience to run the company. So, in 1955, some workers went on strike. During a strike,

Nintendo employees on strike in 1955

people stop working in order to protest what they don't like. To show the protesters who was boss, Hiroshi fired all of them, too!

Although he got off to a rocky start as president, he gained the respect of workers by leading Nintendo to great success. In 1959, he made a deal with the Walt Disney Company. Well-known Disney cartoon characters were featured on Nintendo's plastic playing cards. The deck of cards came with a booklet that gave instructions for different card games. The packs were a very popular and more than six hundred thousand units were sold in the first year.

Walt Disney

That wasn't enough for Hiroshi. He wanted to try other businesses besides cards. He started a taxi service, a chain of hotels, and a TV network. He also tried selling packets of instant rice. None of these businesses, however, were successful, and Hiroshi had to close all of them. At the same time, people were losing interest in playing cards. What would come next for Nintendo?

CHAPTER 2
Let's Have Some Fun!

As luck would have it, in 1965, Nintendo hired an engineer named Gunpei Yokoi. His job was to keep the machinery that made the playing cards working. In his spare time, however, Gunpei liked to make gadgets for his own amusement.

Gunpei Yokoi

One day, Hiroshi walked by Gunpei's office and saw him playing with one of his inventions. It was a mechanical claw that could extend and grab things. Hiroshi thought this would make a great toy. He asked Gunpei to develop it in time to sell for Christmas that year.

The Nintendo Ultra Hand was released in 1966. By 1970, more than one million were sold. Hiroshi now decided that he should forget about trying other businesses and stick to making toys.

Nintendo Ultra Hand

The Holiday Season

Many toy manufacturers aim to get their newest toys into stores during the months of November and December. Since toys are such popular gifts, this is the time of year that sales of toys are at their highest. Often, whether a toy company has a good year depends on how many toys are sold from late October through December.

SHAW'S TOYS
Merry Christmas
Happy Holidays
GAMES
TOYS
GAMES

Hiroshi took Gunpei off the assembly line and made him the head of Nintendo's Research and Development (R&D) Group. This meant Gunpei and his team worked to come up with more new ideas for toys. In 1967, Nintendo released the Ultra Machine. It came with a plastic bat and launched soft baseballs for a player to hit.

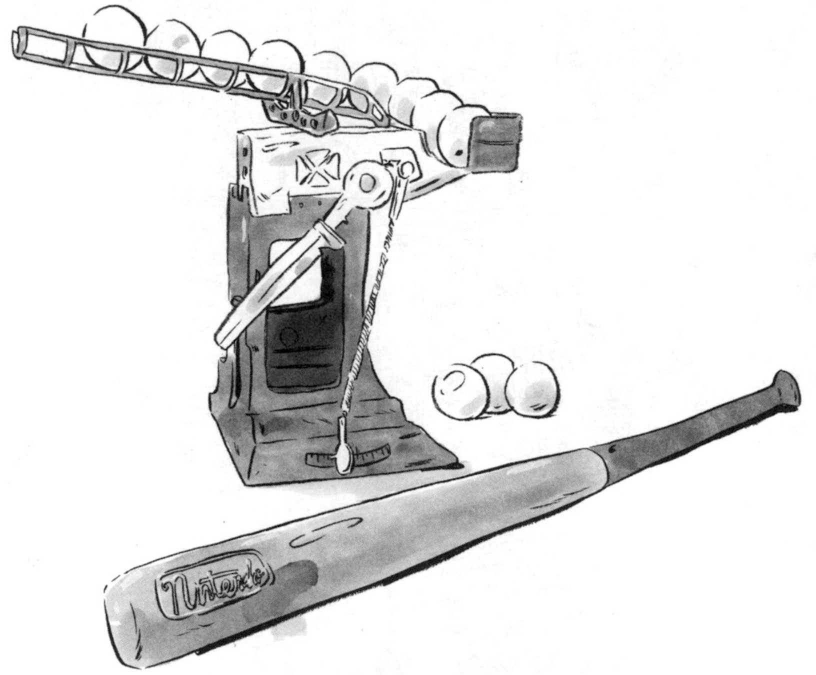

Nintendo Ultra Machine

Nintendo Ultra Scope

In 1971, Gunpei created a periscope called the Ultra Scope. A periscope is an instrument that contains lenses and mirrors that help a person get a view of things that normally they wouldn't be able to see. It's a cool gadget to use for spying!

Soon, Gunpei and his R&D team began using electronics in their toys. Electronics are devices that use electricity to carry or process information. Many products are based on electronics. They include computers, digital cameras, radios, and television sets.

In 1970, Nintendo introduced the Beam Gun series. Toy guns used battery-powered electronics to fire a light at a target. If hit, the target lit up and made sounds. This was the first time in the Japanese toy industry that electronics were used.

Hundreds of thousands of the guns were sold. Nintendo had created something new that both children and adults could enjoy together.

Not every new idea, however, proved to be a success. One day Hiroshi read a newspaper article about clay pigeon shooting. In this sport, a person shoots at clay disks that are launched into the air by a machine. Hiroshi immediately asked Gunpei to create a game based on this sport. Gunpei and his team came up with the Laser Clay Shooting System.

Here's how it worked: On a wall, a film projector cast images of flying clay pigeons into a large woodland scene. Players had to shoot the moving targets with toy light guns. If they hit the target, the projector then showed the image of a "pigeon" falling and kept track of how many had been hit.

Hiroshi wanted to put this game in empty bowling alleys throughout Japan. Bowling, which had once been very popular in Japan, had died out. There were many bowling alleys available for Hiroshi to buy.

The year was 1973, and at first the Laser Clay Shooting System looked like a hit. Nintendo received orders from many other countries in Asia as well. But then the orders stopped coming in and many were canceled. The Laser Clay Shooting System was too expensive. Nintendo lost $64 million!

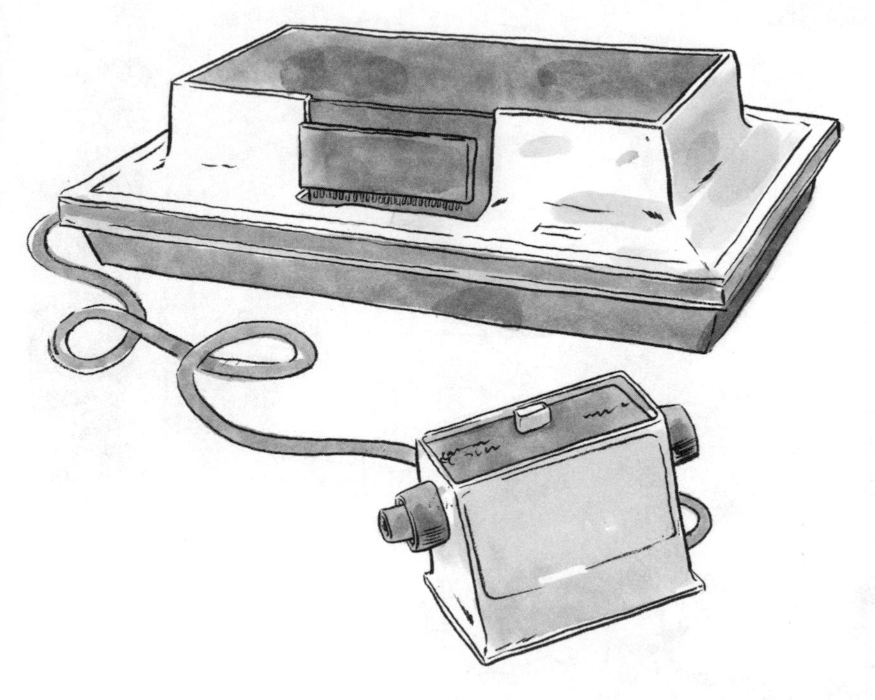

Magnavox Odyssey

During the 1970s, companies such as Atari, Magnavox, Coleco, and Intellivision were making home video consoles (electronic gaming systems) that could be used with TV sets. Hiroshi saw that home video gaming was hot, and he wanted to be part of it. After he got the rights to sell the Magnavox Odyssey in Japan, he was encouraged to take a step further. Nintendo began developing its own video games both for arcades and for homes.

Pong

In 1972, Atari, Inc., an American video game developer, released an arcade game called *Pong*. It was the start of something huge. Although if you looked at *Pong* today, you'd never guess that! This simple table tennis (Ping-Pong) game featured two paddles and a ball on a black screen. The object was to hit the ball back and forth with the paddles until one player missed. That meant a point for the other player. The first one to reach eleven points won the game.

The first *Pong* game was placed in a bar in Sunnyvale, California. It was put on a barrel near a jukebox and pinball machines.

Would people want to play *Pong*?

Yes, they sure did!

Pong was such a hit that it broke down because too many quarters were stuffed into the coin box! The extra coins were not allowing the game to start.

The answer was to make a deeper coin box.

Pong was not the first arcade video game, but it was the first one to become really popular. Soon, more than thirty-five thousand units were sold in the United States. *Pong* made playing video arcade games a new fad.

CHAPTER 3
Nintendo Goes to America

The largest market for video games was North America. Hiroshi knew his company had to get to all those millions of players. So, in 1980, he opened Nintendo of America and, to keep the company all in the family, he made his son-in-law Minoru Arakawa (say: MI-noh-roo ARA-ka-wa) the president of Nintendo of America (NOA).

This new branch of Nintendo started to distribute Game & Watch games throughout the United States. But this didn't lead to the big success Hiroshi had hoped

Minoru Arakawa

for. What the company needed was a hit game.

Did that happen right away?

No.

In Japan, a Nintendo R&D team had been working on a coin-operated arcade game. It was called *Radar Scope*, and the idea of the game was for players to shoot attacking spacecraft. This game became popular in Japan and showed quite a bit of promise in the United States when tested on small audiences.

Minoru placed a big order for the United States. Unfortunately, there were long delays in getting the game made and shipped to New York City. When it finally arrived, arcade owners were extremely disappointed. *Radar Scope* was expensive and—even worse—they thought it was boring and made irritating sounds. *Radar Scope* was a major flop. Nintendo of America was stuck with thousands of unsold units sitting in a warehouse.

Although shaken by this failure, Minoru looked for ways to make up for all the lost money. He wondered whether the problems could be fixed and the games reinstalled into all the cabinets that were unsold.

Shigeru Miyamoto

Back in Japan, a new employee, Shigeru Miyamoto (say: SHI-geh-roo MI-ya-moh-toe) was asked to fix the *Radar Scope* game. But Shigeru thought it would be a much better idea to start from scratch and create something new.

So that's what he did!

CHAPTER 4
Father of Modern Video Games

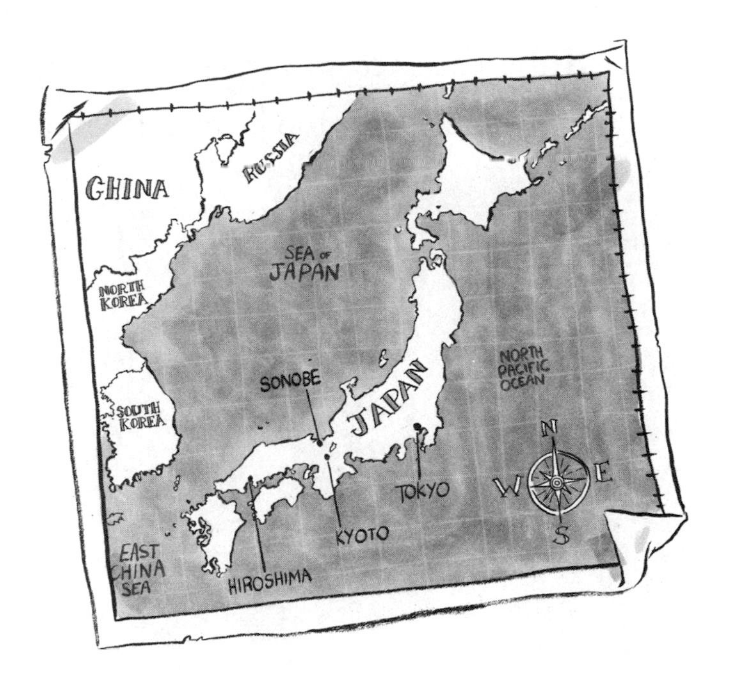

Shigeru Miyamoto was born in Sonobe, a rural town in Japan, in 1952. As a young child, he was full of imagination. He loved doodling, reading, and telling stories. He loved drawing manga, creating cartoon flip books, and putting on puppet shows. He would also go exploring the countryside, biking, walking, climbing trees, and fishing in a nearby stream.

One day, while he was out exploring, he discovered the entrance to a cave. He returned the next day with a lantern so he could explore it.

Shigeru spent many long days exploring this underground cave. One of the things he liked most was the fear and excitement of not knowing what was waiting for him around the bend when he crawled through tunnels. Shigeru never forgot his childhood adventures.

Caution

Entering and exploring a cave alone is never a good idea. It's always best to tour a cave with a grown-up who knows the cave's tunnels and nooks and crannies.

Shigeru spent five years getting a college degree in industrial design. He painted, drew, and built things in his classes. In his free time, one of the things he most enjoyed was playing early video games.

In 1975, Shigeru graduated. Now that he was finished with school, he needed a job. He first thought he would like to become a manga artist. But then he changed his mind and decided he wanted to work making toys.

Through his father, Shigeru was able to get a job interview with Hiroshi Yamauchi. At that time, Hiroshi was more interested in hiring engineers, not artists. But he liked Shigeru and asked him to return with samples of his work.

Shigeru gathered artwork he had done in college, his manga drawings, and his designs for a seesaw that could hold three kids at the same time. He also included his hand-carved colorful children's clothes hangers in the shapes of animals.

When Shigeru returned, Hiroshi liked what he saw. He thought that Shigeru had a childlike way of looking at the world and this was what

Nintendo needed. Hiroshi hired him to be the first artist on Nintendo's staff. Shigeru started in 1977, painting panels for the cabinets of the arcade games.

What Is Manga?

Manga are Japanese comic books and graphic novels that are created for children as well as adults. Manga usually features characters with large eyes, exaggerated emotions, fine features, and colorful hair.

Manga has many genres (genres are literary styles expressed in writing). Some of the genres are action, adventure, comedy, drama, fantasy, historical, mystery, romance, science fiction, and supernatural. The beauty of manga is in the artwork. The art tells most of the story through emotions and actions.

The correct way to read manga is to start at the upper-right corner of the upper-right panel and then read from right to left. Repeat this process until you're done with all the panels in a section. Then move down to the next section of panels and repeat the right-to-left process.

How to read manga

When *Radar Scope* failed in the United States, Shigeru decided to try to develop a completely new game. He didn't like the Ping-Pong and shooting games that were popular at the time. He wanted to design something very different—a game with characters and a storyline.

His idea was to base a game on the characters in the Popeye cartoons, which were very popular in the United States. But Nintendo couldn't make a deal to use them. So, instead, Shigeru created new characters, ones that could jump on-screen. Instead of Popeye, there was now Jumpman (a carpenter). Olive Oyl (Popeye's girlfriend) became Lady (later Pauline), and Bluto (the villain in the Popeye cartoons) became an ape named Donkey Kong. If naming an ape "donkey" seems odd, it's because Shigeru mistakenly thought that in English, "donkey" meant "stupid." Donkey Kong had kidnapped Lady from Jumpman and brought her to a construction site.

The Asahi Shimbun/Getty Images

Nintendo's hanafuda playing-card factory, 1956

The Asahi Shimbun/Getty Images

Hiroshi Yamauchi, Nintendo's third president

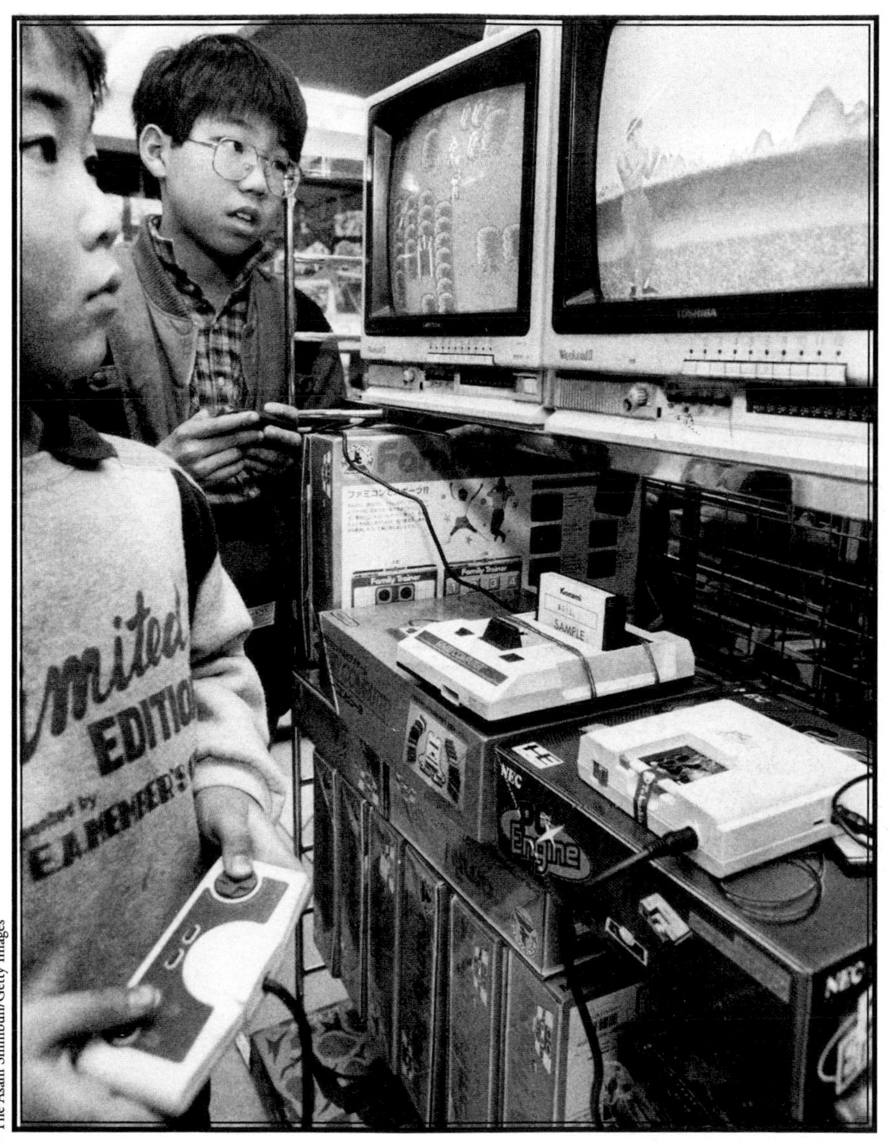

The Asahi Shimbun/Getty Images

Children in Japan playing with one of Nintendo's first gaming systems, 1987

Ralf-Finn Hestoft/Corbis Historical/Getty Images

Shigeru Miyamoto, video game designer and the creator of Mario

James Keyser/The LIFE Images Collection/Getty Images

Nintendo's *Super Mario World* video game

JIMI CELESTE/Patrick McMullan/Getty Images

Mario at the Nintendo *New Super Mario Bros.* Wii launch event

Minoru Arakawa, former president of Nintendo of America

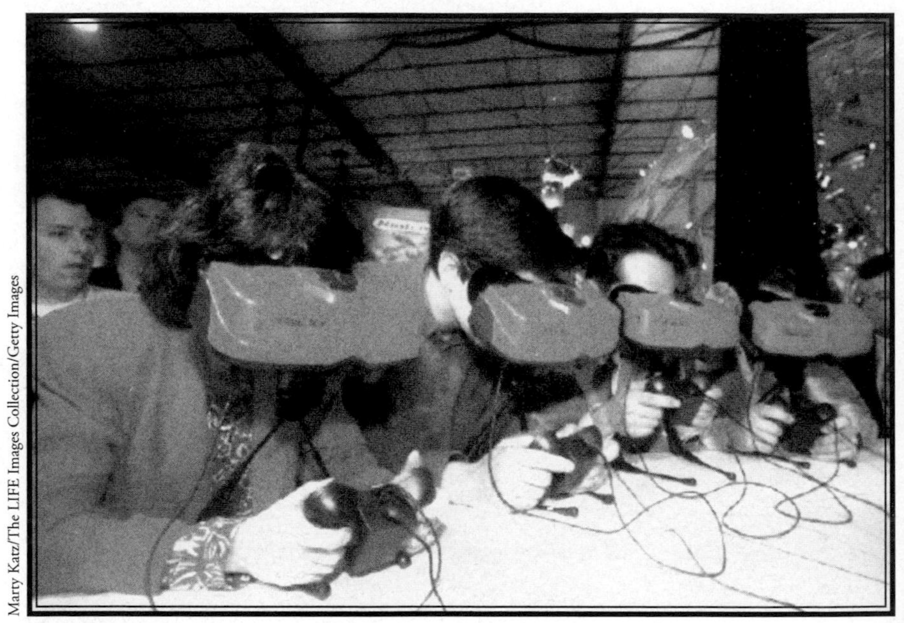

Marty Katz/The LIFE Images Collection/Getty Images

Customers playing with Nintendo's Virtual Boy, 1995

Wojtek Laski/Hulton Archive/Getty Images

Alexey Pajitnov, the creator of the computer game *Tetris*

YOSHIKAZU TSUNO/AFP/Getty Images

Japanese boys with two versions of the new Pokémon video game and their Nintendo Game Boys, 1999

KAZUHIRO NOGI/AFP/Getty Images

Customers buying the Nintendo DS, 2004

Volkan Furuncu/Anadolu Agency/Getty Images

Playing *Pokémon GO* in New York City, 2016

Suzanne Kreiter/Boston Globe/Getty Images

Playing Wii bowling at a senior center

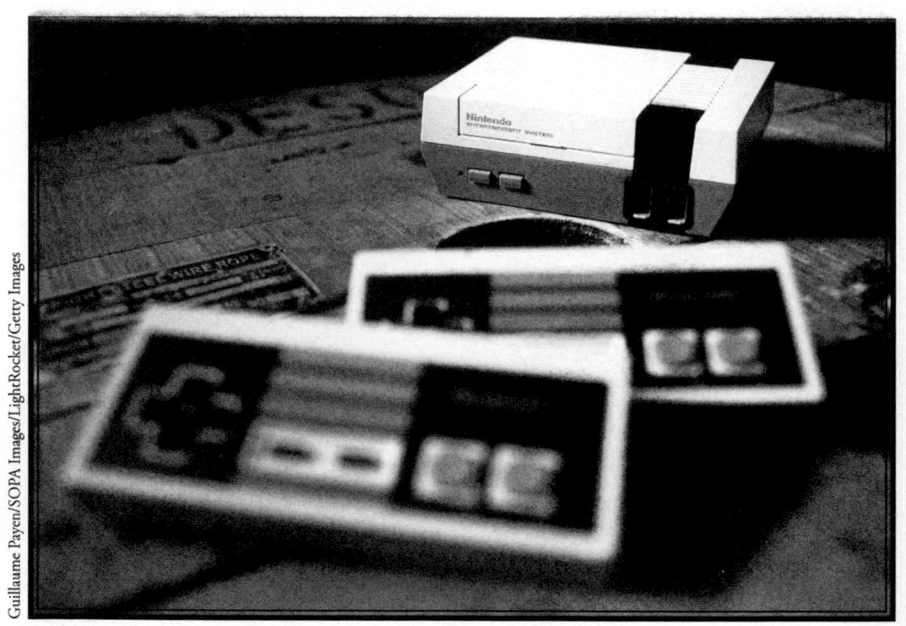

Guillaume Payen/SOPA Images/LightRocker/Getty Images

Nintendo Entertainment System Classic Edition mini console and controllers launched in 2016

Kyodo News Stills/Kyodo News/Getty Images

Customers with Nintendo's new Switch console, 2017

Kiyoshi Ota/Bloomberg/Getty Images

Nintendo headquarters, Kyoto, Japan

The object of the game was for Jumpman to rescue Lady. Game players took on the role of Jumpman.

Donkey Kong was different from other arcade games. Besides telling a story, it is often considered the first true platform game. In a platform game, characters run, jump, or walk over obstacles to reach new levels. (An obstacle prevents players from getting somewhere.)

Jumpman, Donkey Kong, and Lady

Popeye the Sailor Man

Popeye the Sailor Man was introduced in a newspaper comic strip titled *Thimble Theatre* on January 17, 1929. Right away, readers adored Popeye. He was strong and tough, and he never backed down from a challenge. How did he get this way? Popeye ate spinach! Popeye's most famous saying was "I'm strong to da finich 'cause I eats my spinach. I'm Popeye the Sailor Man!" The only thing Popeye loved more than spinach was his girlfriend, Olive Oyl.

Over time, Popeye starred in animated movies, an animated TV series, a radio show, a comic book series, video and pinball games, and a live-action movie.

Popeye, Olive Oyl, and Bluto

As Jumpman moved up ladders and across girders to get to Lady, Donkey Kong rolled barrels to knock down Jumpman. Players had to make Jumpman jump over the barrels.

Shigeru gave Jumpman a red hat and a big mustache. This made Jumpman easy to see on a small screen. Before the game was finished, Minoru Arakawa, the president of Nintendo's US company, changed Jumpman's name to Mario.

Why?

Minoru needed an American name for the character and chose the name of the landlord of Nintendo's Seattle-area warehouse, Mario Segale.

Mario Segale

Once released in 1981, *Donkey Kong* was a tremendous success in Japan and also in the United States. NOA sold the two thousand *Radar Scope* cabinets that had been reprogrammed with *Donkey Kong* and then another sixty thousand in just one year for a total of almost $2 million in sales. Hiroshi finally had what he wanted—a game that broke into the world market.

The D-Pad

When Gunpei Yokoi started working on the *Donkey Kong* Game & Watch, he wanted it to be just like the *Donkey Kong* arcade game. But he realized that the joystick used on arcade games was too large for this handheld device, and it would be difficult to carry it around. Gunpei worked hard on this problem and finally came up with the D-pad, or directional pad. This was a huge invention that made all future handheld gaming devices and consoles possible. The D-pad took up less space and eliminated the need for a joystick.

Mario became the star of *Donkey Kong* and many more Nintendo games. Today he is recognized around the world and has become the company's mascot.

Shigeru is considered the father of video gaming and the greatest video game designer in

the world. He has helped make more than 150 games. *Donkey Kong* reflected everything that Nintendo stands for as a company—humorous, nonviolent family entertainment for both kids and adults.

Nintendo's Graphics

Nintendo's graphics are known to be colorful, smart, and fun. As video game technology improved, Shigeru was able to make his characters and the games themselves more complex. For instance, Mario started out looking very flat and boxy. Over time, he turned into a character that looks three-dimensional.

Original Mario

CHAPTER 5
Crash!

Things were certainly looking up for Nintendo. In the early 1980s, the home video game industry was booming in North America. Everyone wanted to play the games, and now people could do that right on their TV screens. Also, the price of home consoles had dropped, so more people could afford them.

And then, suddenly, it all came crashing down. There were three main reasons why.

First, gamers had dozens of different home consoles to choose from. Each console came with its own set of games. But games from other companies could also be played on all consoles. The North American market was flooded with dozens of consoles, giving consumers way too many choices.

Second, because of the high demand for more video games, many were rushed out. They weren't fun to play and ended up being huge flops. For example, the movie *E.T.—The Extra-Terrestrial*

was a megahit. Yet Atari's video game version of the movie is considered by many to be the worst video game of all time. By the time Atari made a deal to create a video game based on the popular alien, the designer only had *five weeks* to develop it. Video games usually take months or even years to make. Gamers disliked the graphics and found the game extremely difficult to play. It hardly sold during the 1982 holiday season.

E.T.—The Extra-Terrestrial

And a third reason for the crash was that by 1983, the price of home computers had dropped. More and more people could afford to own one. A home computer was now about the same price as a gaming console. A computer could do much more than just play video games. But a video console could *only* play games, nothing more. So, many people bought a home computer instead of a home console.

After a while, toy stores decided that video gaming was over. They stopped selling the games. For the next three years, sales of video games were at an all-time low. Atari, the leader of the gaming industry at the time, nearly went out of business.

Where Have All the Cartridges Gone?

The crash left many companies with tons of game cartridges and consoles that could not be sold. To get rid of all their unsold merchandise, Atari ended up burying it in a landfill in Alamogordo, New Mexico.

Many people never believed any burial had taken place. They thought it was a tall tale. Then, in 2014,

a documentary film was made called *Atari: Game Over.* Part of it shows discarded games and hardware being uncovered.

Atari officials said nearly 800,000 cartridges of various games had been buried, including *E.T.* But a much smaller number, 1,178 games for the Atari 2600 console, were dug up.

Nintendo was more fortunate than Atari. Hiroshi had already created a home console system. In 1985, he released the Nintendo Entertainment System (NES) in the United States and advertised it as a control deck instead of a video game console.

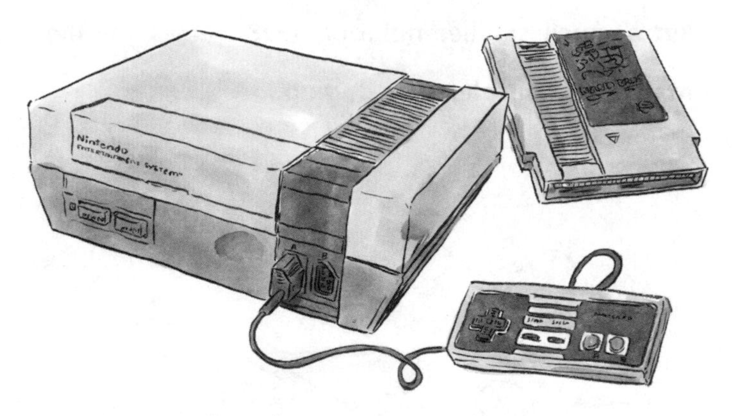

Nintendo Entertainment System

Why was that important?

Nintendo realized that the gaming industry was moving away from game consoles and toward home computers. The NES is thought to have been based on the style of a modern VCR (the cartridge was loaded into a door at the front of the NES) instead of a top-loaded video game console. Nintendo also added a lockout chip in the NES. This made sure that low-quality games from other companies wouldn't work on it.

Were sales great in the beginning?

No.

But that all changed in 1986 when Shigeru produced a multi-level adventure game called *Super Mario Bros.* Nintendo included it with the NES in the United States. *Super Mario Bros.* became the best-selling video game of its time.

What made it so popular?

It was so different and so much fun to play! Players could make Mario stomp on mushrooms, flip fireballs, and save the princess no matter where she was—and she was always in a different castle throughout the game. *Super Mario Bros.* allowed gamers to take part in an adventure in a whole new world and to unlock new stages as they played. And, *Super Mario Bros.* could be played again and again, and it would be different for players each time.

The NES was a huge hit in the United States, and as of 1986, in Europe, too. Between 1985 and 1988, Shigeru created some of the most popular games of all time for the NES. One example was the fantasy action-adventure *The Legend of Zelda*.

Much of the game centers on exploring various caves around Death Mountain. The dungeon in the game is a series of chambers connected by different paths, just like the cave system Shigeru explored as a young boy.

The Legend of Zelda also introduced a new type of gameplay that would eventually become a standard in video games. Instead of scoring points and winning a game based on a high score, the goal of *The Legend of Zelda* was to interact with the characters and reach the end of an epic story. It was about the thrill of discovery! *The Legend of Zelda* also came with a new feature: Players could now save their place in a game.

In 1988 alone, Nintendo released sixty-five titles for its NES game library, and Nintendo was *the* number one company in the video game industry around the world. Nintendo helped breathe new life into video game playing!

Nintendo Power Magazine

In July 1988, the first issue of *Nintendo Power* magazine came out. The cover showed Mario from *Super Mario Bros. 2*. More than 3.5 million fans got the magazine, which was published every other month. It had articles about upcoming new games and when they would be released. It gave tips and secrets for playing current games, and fan letters were shared in each issue. In 1991, it became a monthly magazine. After twenty-four years and 285 issues, *Nintendo Power* ended in December 2012.

CHAPTER 6
Game Boy

The Nintendo Entertainment System was selling extremely well around the world. But Hiroshi was always looking for ways to make Nintendo even better. Since 1987, Gunpei and his R&D team had been working on a new gaming device. It would be handheld and easy to carry like the Game & Watch. But it would also have interchangeable cartridges and a similar button layout to the *Donkey Kong* Game & Watch. In addition, Gunpei wanted the device to be sturdy, low priced, and have a long battery life.

Nintendo Game Boy

The result was the Game Boy.

The Game Boy came out in Japan on April 21, 1989. It had these games: *Super Mario Land*, *Alleyway*, *Baseball*, and *Yakuman*. Three months later, on July 31, 1989, the Game Boy was launched in North America. It was bundled with a new game called *Tetris*.

Tetris was not created in Japan or North America. *Tetris* came from Russia. Alexey Pajitnov (say: ah-LEK-say pah-JEET-nov) was a computer programmer who worked at a government computer center in Moscow.

Alexey Pajitnov

As a child, he had always loved puzzles, especially pentominoes.

A set of pentominoes consists of twelve shapes made by joining five squares together side-to-side.

Set of pentominoes

In June 1984, Alexey got the idea that this game might make a fun computer game. He quickly realized, though, that twelve pentomino pieces rotating on a small screen would be too complicated. So, he reduced the pieces to seven shapes made by joining four squares together side-to-side.

Alexey wrote the original program on a Russian computer. It did not have graphics, so he used letters for the playing pieces. Then he figured out how to make the pieces flip and rotate. Alexey programmed the game so that each full line of pieces would disappear and give the player more space on the screen to continue playing. As players reached different levels, the pieces appeared faster and faster. Alexey named the game *Tetris*,

taking the first part of the Greek word *tetra*, which means "four," and the second part of the word *tennis*, which was Alexey's favorite sport.

Alexey worked for the Russian government when he created the game. And he worried he might get in trouble if he tried to sell it himself. So, he granted his rights to the government for ten years. Boy, was the country lucky! Alexey did not make any money from the sales of *Tetris* until 1996.

Today, *Tetris* is among the top-selling games of all time and one of the most well-known in the world. There are several reasons for this. It is a simple game to learn, so many people are willing to try it. (It's hard, however, to get really skillful at it.) *Tetris* holds players' attention for long periods of time. Gamers always feel as though they learn something new as they play. It also has good pacing. It starts slow, then goes faster and faster to keep players on their toes!

The Game Boy was a huge success in North America. It sold more than 118 million units *and* adults bought the Game Boy, too. They played on their way to and from work. Video games were no longer just for kids!

Another Flop

Gunpei Yokoi and his R&D team worked for many years on a portable game console that could display 3-D (three-dimensional) graphics. It was called Virtual Boy. It was released in 1995 and was one of Nintendo's worst failures. Gamers complained of eyestrain, headaches, motion sickness, and vomiting from the wraparound headset and the black-and-red graphics. The Virtual Boy was discontinued about a year after it came out.

It was among the last products Gunpei Yokoi worked on at Nintendo. He also helped with the Game Boy Pocket before leaving the company in 1996. Gunpei started his own toy company but, sadly, he was killed in a car accident the next year.

CHAPTER 7
Mario vs. Sonic

By 1990, nine out of every ten video games sold were made by Nintendo! But Sega, a rival company from the early days of arcade games, was getting ready to battle Nintendo for the top spot in the gaming world.

It was in 1989 that Sega released its own popular home video game console, the sixteen-bit Sega Genesis. This system included super-detailed graphics, extremely vibrant colors, and complex games. In 1992, Sega surpassed Nintendo in sales. The video game war between Nintendo and Sega would last for the next ten years.

The two companies had completely different ideas about their products.

For Nintendo, the quality of their games was most important. They chose to produce far fewer new games than Sega, but the Nintendo games were better. Sega, on the other hand, believed in quantity. They produced an extremely large number of games. Many were flops, but even if only a few were hits, that was enough for Sega to make money.

Sega wanted to create games based on pop culture, trends, gamers' interests, and art. Their games were edgy and fast-paced and included violent content. Sega targeted an older audience while Nintendo continued selling its kid-friendly games to boys ages six to twelve. Nintendo had a strict policy about no violence in their games in keeping with their family-friendly image.

Sega wanted a mascot that could compete with Nintendo's Mario. They came up with Sonic, a speedy blue hedgehog with lots of attitude. Sonic was designed to be faster, more dangerous, and cooler than Mario. Sega used Sonic to promote its products, and soon he became a well-known character.

Nintendo concentrated on developing games rather than focusing on advertising. Sega's ads often poked fun at Nintendo and attempted to portray Nintendo as a toymaker that was behind the times. Sega aimed to appeal to older gamers who wanted something cooler.

Nintendo's answer to the Sega Genesis was their sixteen-bit Super Nintendo Entertainment System (SNES), which was released in 1991 in North America. *Super Mario World* came with this console. Other launch games included *F-Zero*, *Pilotwings*, and *SimCity*. In time, the SNES landed Sega in the number two spot again.

And early in 2001, Sega stopped making game consoles altogether. After that, it just concentrated on creating new games.

In 1996, in Japan, Nintendo released *Pokémon* (also known as *Pocket Monsters*), a role-playing game. A role-playing game (RPG) is a kind of game where the player controls a fictional character (or characters) that goes on a quest in an imaginary world. In the Pokémon games, players must catch and train Pokémon creatures to battle one another. The battles are the main theme of the games, but players also need to reach certain objectives within the game.

Pikachu from Pokémon

Pokémon was an instant success. Nintendo didn't think the game would work in the American market but tried it there anyway. As in Japan, Pokémon came with games, trading cards, a TV show, comics, movies, and toys. To roll out the game, NOA used this simple hook—collectability. The famous slogan was "Gotta Catch 'Em All!"

Violence in Video Games

Throughout the history of video gaming, there has been much controversy about the violence in video games. Here are the guidelines that were established by the Entertainment Software Rating Board (ESRB):

- E is for "everyone." Suitable for all ages. May contain minimal violence, some comic mischief, and/or mild language.
- E10+ is for "everyone ages ten and older." Titles in this category may contain more cartoon, fantasy, or mild violence, mild language, and/or minimal suggestive themes.
- T is for "teen." May be suitable for ages thirteen and up. May contain violent content, mild or strong language, and/or suggestive themes.
- M is for "mature." May be suitable for persons ages seventeen and up. May contain mature

sexual themes, more intense violence, and/or strong language.

- AO is for "adults only." Content is suitable only for adults. May include graphic depictions of sex and/or violence. Adults Only products are not intended for persons under the age of eighteen.
- RP is for "rating pending." Titles have been submitted and are awaiting final rating.

The ESRB also suggests that children discuss with parents and/or caregivers which games are appropriate for them to play.

NOA spent $15 million to $20 million on its marketing campaign. This was something the company normally didn't do. This was more the way Sega worked when it brought out a new product. Nintendo sent a videotape explaining Pokémon to all the subscribers of their *Nintendo Power* magazine. The video spelled out the whole concept of Pokémon and announced that there

would be Game Boy games, toys, card games, and a TV show.

The marketing campaign worked. *Pokémon Red* and *Pokémon Blue* were released in North America in 1998 and sold four hundred thousand copies in less than a month. The Red and Blue games each have several exclusive Pokémon, which means that players have to trade with one another.

The national TV show debuted in September 1998, and in November 1999, *Pokémon: The First Movie* opened at the top of the box office. By the end of 1999, Pokémon was making seven billion dollars around the globe. Today, it's still played by millions of gamers!

CHAPTER 8
Games for the Whole Family

Competition from Sega wasn't nearly as fierce anymore. But between the mid-1990s and the mid-2000s, Sony's PlayStation consoles and Microsoft's Xbox console were on the rise, and Nintendo was losing ground once again. Every new Nintendo console since the NES had sold fewer than the system before it. And, in 2002,

PlayStation 2 and Xbox consoles

Satoru Iwata

both Hiroshi Yamauchi (president of Nintendo for fifty-two years) and Minoru Arakawa (president of NOA for twenty-two years) retired. This ended the Yamauchi family's control of the company. The new president, Satoru Iwata (say: SA-toh-roo EE-wah-ta), became the fourth president of Nintendo.

Hiroshi died on September 19, 2013, at the age of eighty-five.

When Hiroshi left Nintendo, his parting words to Satoru were to create a Game Boy with two screens. Nintendo's research had shown that the gap between gamers and non-gamers was widening. Complicated controls put off non-gamers and made them dislike video games even more. So, Satoru Iwata and Shigeru Miyamoto decided to make this latest handheld device as simple as possible.

In November 2004, the Nintendo DS (DS stands for "Dual Screen") came out in the United States. The DS had two LCD screens and a built-in microphone. The bottom screen was a touchscreen, which made controlling games easier than ever before. The DS also featured wireless multiplayer communication. This allowed a player to connect with other players' systems within range without the use of the internet.

Satoru and Shigeru hoped that young children, parents, and grandparents, along with Nintendo's core gamers, would want to play it. And with games like *Nintendogs*, where you train and care for a virtual dog of your choosing, and *Brain Age: Train Your Brain in Minutes a Day!*, to help keep your brain sharp, the DS appealed to a much wider age range of gamers.

The original DS sold 18.79 million units. The DS handheld consoles are the best-selling handheld product line for Nintendo.

Nintendo was on a roll. In November 2006, the company launched a whole new gaming system—the Wii home console.

The console, which was compact and portable, came with a Wii remote and a nunchuk. The nunchuk was used as a control stick for some games and was connected to the remote with a long cord that allowed a player to have more control over it. The Wii remote was wireless and could be held with one hand. And with special new sensor technology, the Wii put players right into the game. Players' gestures—their swings and swipes—controlled the characters on-screen so that they moved in the exact same way. Holding the Wii remote in the game of golf, a player used a side-to-side motion to putt the ball into the hole. Like the DS, the Wii was designed for lifelong gamers as well as people who had never, or rarely ever, played a video game.

The Top Ten Best-Selling Nintendo DS Games

1. *New Super Mario Bros.*
2. *Nintendogs*
3. *Mario Kart DS*
4. *Brain Age: Train Your Brain in Minutes a Day!*
5. *Pokémon Diamond* and *Pearl*
6. *Pokémon Black* and *White*
7. *Brain Age 2: Train Your Brain in More Minutes a Day!*
8. *Pokémon HeartGold* and *SoulSilver*
9. *Animal Crossing: Wild World*
10. *Super Mario 64 DS*

Every Wii console sold in North America was bundled with the *Wii Sports* game, which included five different sports—golf, tennis, baseball, bowling, and boxing. The nunchuk was only used with the boxing game.

The Wii had broad appeal and wound up in retirement homes and in office staff rooms as well as in family dens. Wherever people wanted to get exercise indoors or just have fun, there was a Wii! By December 2008, the Wii had sold more than 44 million units worldwide—one and a half times as many as Microsoft's Xbox 360 and twice as many as Sony's PlayStation 3. It became Nintendo's best-selling home console of all time in the United States, Japan, and Europe. Nintendo was back on top!

As had happened so often in its history, Nintendo followed up all this success with another huge flop—the Wii U of 2012 turned out to be another of Nintendo's big failures.

Its marketing plan was confusing. Many gamers thought it was a handheld system instead of a new home console system. And some thought it was an add-on to the original Wii. The Wii U sold less than 14 million units compared to the Wii's 101 million units sold by the end of 2016. Nintendo stopped making the Wii U in January 2017.

Wii U

By March 2017, Nintendo was ready with another new home console, the Nintendo Switch. This console could be hooked up to a television or used as a handheld device.

Nintendo Switch

As of February 2019, the Switch was the fastest-selling home console in both Japan and the United States, and it remained the top-selling video game console in the United States through October 2019.

Throughout its very long history, Nintendo experienced high points and low points in its business, much like gamers do when playing video games. Just when Nintendo was at the top of the industry, an obstacle would come along and knock them down, but the company always learned from its mistakes and resumed its position as an industry leader time and time again.

CHAPTER 9
The Power of Nintendo

Nintendo's impact around the world has been enormous. Hiroshi Yamauchi took over a small company that produced playing cards and

turned it into a worldwide video game giant. Nintendo's ability to create ever cooler gadgets while also bringing out new family-friendly games was the basis for this company's success.

There's no doubt that Nintendo truly knows its audience. In 2016, the company brought back its incredibly popular NES console in a miniature version of the original. This was aimed at older fans who remembered NES from their childhoods as well as gamers who missed out on its initial release. It cost sixty dollars and came with thirty

classic NES games including *Super Mario Bros.*, *The Legend of Zelda*, and *Donkey Kong*. It was a limited edition that was out for less than half a year. A runaway hit, it was nearly impossible to find because it sold out so quickly.

It will be exciting to see what comes next!

A Note to Readers

Playing video games is a lot of fun, and it's natural that some kids want to share their enthusiasm with other gamers. There are many chat rooms and fan pages online where players discuss games and tips. If you ever want to participate in something like this, make sure you first have approval from a parent or trusted grown-up. Also, remember that conversations should be about games—never give out personal information about yourself.

Timeline of Nintendo

1889	Nintendo is founded by Fusajiro Yamauchi
1949	Hiroshi Yamauchi becomes president of Nintendo
1966	Nintendo enters the toy market by releasing Gunpei Yokoi's Ultra Hand in Japan
1970	Nintendo's Beam Gun series are its first toys with electronics
1977	Hiroshi Yamauchi hires Shigeru Miyamoto as the first staff artist for Nintendo
1980	Yamauchi opens Nintendo of America (NOA)
1981	*Donkey Kong* is released as an arcade game
1985	The Nintendo Entertainment System (NES) is released in the United States
1989	The Game Boy is launched with the game *Tetris* in North America
1991	Super Nintendo Entertainment System (SNES) is released in the United States
1993	Live-action film *Super Mario Bros.* is released in theaters
1997	Gunpei Yokoi dies
2004	The Nintendo DS is released
2006	The Wii home console is released
2017	The Nintendo Switch is released

Timeline of the World

1888	George Eastman invents the Kodak camera and photographic film that comes in a roll
1891	The zipper is invented by Whitcomb Judson
1895	Guglielmo Marconi invents a system of wireless communication using radio waves
1949	RCA releases the first 45 rpm record
1957	The first PC (personal computer), the IBM 610, is invented
1966	Filmmaker and animator Walt Disney dies on December 15
1967	First human heart transplant is performed in South Africa
1970	The pocket calculator is invented in Japan
1983	Compact discs (CDs) are launched as a new way to store music by the Sony and Philips corporations
1984	The first commercially available cell phone is created by Motorola
1990	The first page is posted on the World Wide Web
1995	DVD, a digital optical disc storage format, is invented and developed by Philips, Sony, Toshiba, and Panasonic
2007	Apple introduces the first iPhone
2010	3-D TV starts to become more widely available
2017	Ten years after the Great Recession started, global economic growth picks up

Bibliography

***Books for young readers**

BBC. "Nintendo Consoles: A History in Pictures." Posted January 13, 2017. https://www.bbc.com/news/technology-38595543.

Cohen, D. S. "The History of Nintendo Video Games: From Playing Cards to the Nintendo Switch." ***Lifewire***. Last updated June 24, 2019. https://www.lifewire.com/history-of-nintendo-729734/.

*Cornell, Kari. ***Nintendo Video Game Designer: Shigeru Miyamoto***. STEM Trailblazer Bios. Minneapolis: Lerner Publications, 2016.

*Hennessey, Jonathan. ***The Comic Book Story of Video Games: The Incredible History of the Electronic Gaming Revolution***. Berkeley, CA: Ten Speed Press, 2017.

Jones, Tegan. "The Surprisingly Long History of Nintendo." ***Gizmodo.*** Posted September 20, 2013. https://gizmodo.com/the-surprisingly-long-history-of-nintendo-1354286257/.

Kent, Steven L. ***The Ultimate History of Video Games***. New York: Three Rivers Press, 2001.

Nintendo. "Nintendo History." https://www.nintendo.co.uk/Corporate/Nintendo-History/Nintendo-History-625945.html.

Ryan, Jeff. ***Super Mario: How Nintendo Conquered America***. New York: Portfolio/Penguin, 2011.

Schkolnick, Matt. "History of Nintendo." **Geeks.** Posted 2016. https://geeks.media/history-of-nintendo/.

Sheff, David. ***Game Over: How Nintendo Conquered the World***. New York: Vintage Books, 1994.

Stevenson Company. "A Brief History of Nintendo." stevensoncompany.com/nintendo-brief-history.

*Sutherland, Adam. ***The Story of Nintendo***. The Business of High Tech. New York: Rosen Publishing Group, 2012.

*Thomas, Rachael L. ***Nintendo Innovator: Hiroshi Yamauchi***. Toy Trailblazers. Minneapolis: Abdo Publishing, 2019.

World Video Game Hall of Fame. ***A History of Video Games in 64 Objects.*** New York: HarperCollins, 2018.